Landings
INTERNATIONAL

Training and Program Guide

A Paulist Ministry of Reconciliation

For more information contact:

LANDINGS International
North American Paulist Center
3015 Fourth Street NE
Washington, DC 20017
202-269-2550

LANDINGSdc@yahoo.com
www.landingsintl.org

To order materials:

Paulist Press
997 Macarthur Boulevard
Mahwah, New Jersey 07430
800-218-1903
201-825-7300

info@paulistpress.com
www.paulistpress.com

Revised 2012

ISBN: 978-0-8091-9686-9

Published by Paulist Press, Inc.

Printed and bound in the United States of America

LANDINGS

TRAINING AND PROGRAM GUIDE

edited by
Thomas A. Kane, CSP

Landings INTERNATIONAL
A Paulist Ministry of Reconciliation

Paulist Press
New York / Mahwah, NJ

†

For Jac and Jim

We especially remember the legacy of the late Father Jac Campbell, CSP, the founder of LANDINGS, whose heart for those away from the Church inspired him to start LANDINGS many years ago, and the late Father James Moran, CSP, who continued his work. May our ministry continue to reflect their compassionate vision.

Acknowledgments

Thank you to all who contributed to this revised program:
Anna LaNave, Patricia Watson, Camille Bissmeyer, Karen Vittone,
Steve Petroff, Susan Timoney, and Georgina Vaca

CONTENTS

INTRODUCTION

"The harvest is plenty, but the laborers are few...
Be not afraid...Leave the ninety-nine...
And come with me into the fields..."

LANDINGS, a Paulist program for returning Catholics, is an evangelization and reconciliation process that will help you and your faith community welcome inactive Catholics who want to take another look at the Church. Returnees are part of our Catholic family, and it is important to celebrate their sacred moment of return by giving them "a safe place to land." We find that the LANDINGS process is also an enriching faith experience for active Catholics willing to help.

LANDINGS is both subtle and simple. Since 1989, the lay-oriented process has successfully brought returning Catholics back to active participation in the faith. Many LANDINGS "graduates" go on to become some of the most active members of the community.

We know the harvest is plenty. According to recent surveys, there are almost 65 million Catholics in the United States, but of those Catholics only 36 percent attend Mass on a weekly basis. That means that over 40 million Catholics are potential LANDINGS participants. Trust the Holy Spirit to guide you as you set up your LANDINGS program, and pray that motivated, sincere people will become involved in it.

Be not afraid of—

- Being burdened with another program that will overtax your staff and clergy
- Lacking enough formal knowledge and language to talk about your faith
- Welcoming some who are wounded, searching, and wondering

LANDINGS has welcomed over 1.5 million people in the last twenty years, and we have learned the following:

- Volunteer Catholic laity, with minimum involvement by professional staff and clergy, do very well in welcoming back returning Catholics.
- Catholic laity, when encouraged to be honest, speak with remarkable clarity about their faith. This is an experience of faith sharing, not a religious education course. After completing the LANDINGS program, many returnees who are welcomed back to the Church want to grow in their faith and will then seek out more formal courses in contemporary spirituality and theology.
- Welcoming the returning Catholic is a critical ministry. It is about listening with your heart, hearing the stories of returnees, and warmly welcoming them home to Christ and the Church. Be yourself and be authentic.

The *training section* of this guide describes the step-by-step process of training a LANDINGS team, providing proven practical tips, first for efficient preplanning and then for keeping the process and the volunteers on track and on time during the day itself. The guide also contains the actual script of the training-program DVD that is included in the packet.

The training day is designed to assist the participants in developing ministerial skills and enhancing the art of compassionate listening. During the training, your team will conduct a mock LANDINGS meeting. This is a wonderful opportunity for the entire group to hear the spiritual journeys of each other and to bond as a team before reaching out to the returnees. By the end of the training day, the team will be well equipped to engage in the LANDINGS ministry.

The *program section* of this guide outlines the entire LANDINGS session and assists the program facilitator in organizing and leading each meeting with confidence. The format is simple and direct.

The success of LANDINGS comes from the welcoming spirit and compassion you bring to this needed ministry. Please contact us if you have any questions or need any help with your ministry. Happy LANDINGS!

LANDINGS International
202-269-2550
LANDINGSdc@yahoo.com
www.landingsintl.org

PART I
LANDINGS TRAINING GUIDE

The LANDINGS program facilitator and the welcoming team reflect the unconditional love and acceptance of Christ to a small group of returning Catholics as they reexamine their faith and place in the Church. The program facilitator leads the LANDINGS meetings and strives to create an environment of mutual respect, confidentiality, and sharing. Reconciliation is a work of the Holy Spirit, and the LANDINGS team humbly accepts their role of walking alongside the returnees as they journey together.

Following are key steps and useful tips for organizing a training program:

THE WELCOME TEAM

The first step is to gather the welcome team. Members of the welcome team, who have been selected by the pastor, pastoral leader, and/or coordinator, need to be open, compassionate, and great at listening. The team should represent a wide diversity of ages and life situations. It is very beneficial if at least some team members are returning Catholics themselves. For more information, see "Finding Members for Your Welcome Team" in the *Coordinator's Guide*.

The program facilitator will convene the group, explain the process, and review the program guidelines. The facilitator will explain that team members must participate in a formal LANDINGS training session or have been a member of a previous LANDINGS group, and that the training includes a mock LANDINGS meeting. The program—and perhaps even the training itself—may at first seem too challenging, but assure the members of the welcome team that they will gradually develop confidence through the training and first meeting.

If this is the first time your faith community is using the LANDINGS program, the entire welcome team will need special training. However, as new members join the welcome team after your first session, they too must be trained, unless they have already participated in the program as a returnee. It is advisable not to drop a new, untrained volunteer into an existing welcome team, no matter how experienced that team is. Training is essential, especially in helping the new team member speak comfortably about his or her faith.

TEAM TRAINING

The LANDINGS packet contains a training DVD and its script that will direct you and your team through the entire training day. Think of this training as a mini-retreat, where the team will get to know each other and become comfortable with the LANDINGS process.

Allow at least five hours with breaks for lunch and snacks. Because of this length, the training day is often held on a Saturday. Attendance at the workshop is mandatory for every team member. We also encourage you to invite your pastor or pastoral leader, pastoral staff, and anyone else who might be interested in understanding and assisting with LANDINGS. It is best to schedule your welcome-team training at least six weeks before the beginning of your first session. There will be time to plan the LANDINGS marketing campaign at the training day.

PREPLANNING CHECKLIST

At least a week before the training meeting, make sure these essentials are in place:

√ Check out the space assignment. As a parish program, LANDINGS helps returnees to become familiar with the local church and its offerings; therefore, it is recommended that groups meet in a parish space for the first few meetings. Select a room in a quiet section of the building, so that you will not be interrupted by foot traffic.

√ Make sure there is a working monitor to show the training DVD.

√ Assemble a large writing board, small prayer table, candle, crucifix, Bible, nametags, and markers.

√ Plan refreshments for breaks.

√ Provide lunch, or provide just drinks and dessert and have participants bring their own lunch.

√ Make copies of the DVD training script and the LANDINGS meeting schedule. Each workshop attendee should have a script and a schedule.

√ Make copies of the flyer, the LANDINGS Web page, bulletin announcements, and other resources from the *Coordinator's Guide* to share during the marketing discussion. Again, each workshop attendee should have a copy.

√ View the video before the training so that you understand the exercises. As part of the training, you will conduct a mock LANDINGS meeting. If you have more than ten people, plan on dividing them into small groups during this exercise. Each group should meet in a separate room set up with a circle of chairs.

RECRUITING LEADERS FROM THE WELCOME TEAM

During the training day, the program facilitator runs the mock meeting, following a modified LANDINGS meeting schedule: check-in, opening prayer, storytelling, response to story, discussion of theme, wrap-up reflection, and closing prayer. For the discussion, use "Why Follow Jesus?"—one of the themes in the *Participant's Journal*. The program facilitator needs to prepare the wrap-up reflection beforehand, as well as the closing prayer.

In addition, you will need to recruit two leaders from the welcome team willing to take on these key roles for the training day:

• *Storyteller*. Each meeting, a returnee or a member of the welcome team shares the story of his or her personal faith journey. For the training day, one person per small group is needed to serve as the storyteller for the mock LANDINGS meeting. A week or so ahead of time, provide that person with a copy of "Guidance for Storytelling" (which is immediately after this checklist), so that he or she will be prepared to share in their small group for about twenty minutes.

• *Opening prayer leader*. Each meeting, a returnee or a member of the welcome team leads the group in an opening prayer. The prayer should be based on the guidelines in the *Participant's Journal*, which provide enough suggestions that most people will find something they will be comfortable with. For the training day, one person per small group is needed to serve as the opening prayer leader for the mock meeting. He or she should prepare a simple, five-minute opening prayer.

GUIDANCE FOR STORYTELLING

This is an invitation to you to tell your story. We, the Christian community, need to hear your part of our common faith story. Share with us how God has been active in your life. Use the questions or themes that are most meaningful to you. Begin with a word or two about the faith lives of your parents and grandparents. Consider what important events, people, or situations have shaped your life. Start at the beginning, or start halfway through, or start in the present and flash backward. Do whatever works best. And share only as much as you feel comfortable telling the group.

The following reflection questions are meant to help you tell your story:

- What was your early Church experience?
- What provoked you to leave the Church?
- What were some of the good times and bad times, the highs and lows in your journey?
- Can you name the hunger, the sense of loss, the "something hoped for" that you felt?
- What drew you to or back to the Church?
- Who and what helped you on the return journey? Who and what did not help?
- From where do you draw strength?

CHECKLIST FOR THE DAY BEFORE TRAINING

The day before the workshop, do as much as possible beforehand. It will make the training itself go smoothly and help decrease your stress and any welcome-team jitters.

√ Prepare the main room to simulate a LANDINGS meeting by setting up a circle of chairs around a small central prayer table with a Bible and candle on it.

√ Set up break-out rooms as needed, depending on the number of attendees, for the mock meeting.

√ Organize the handouts, training scripts, and *Participant's Journal*s for use during the workshop. The *Participant's Journal*s will be collected at the end of the day for use by returnees and members of the welcome team during the actual meetings.

√ Check that the monitor to view the DVD is functioning.

√ Call the pastor, pastoral leader, and/or program coordinator to confirm the time that they are expected to arrive.

√ Call any committee members who are contributing in some way (for example, whoever is handling lunch and/or refreshments) to confirm the time.

√ Call the volunteer opening prayer leader and the volunteer storyteller to give them last-minute encouragement and to verify that they will be attending the training.

TRAINING DAY SCHEDULE

9:30–10:00 a.m.	Registration / nametags / refreshments
10:00–10:15 a.m.	Introductions by coordinator or pastor, and explanation why LANDINGS was selected for your faith community Read aloud the Preamble from the *Participant's Journal* to get in the spirit of LANDINGS. Emphasize compassionate listening. Remind the team about confidentiality.
10:15–11:20 a.m.	Start the training DVD Exercise: Your team's story (20 minutes) Exercise: Opening prayer experience (15 minutes)
11:20 AM–12:40 p.m.	Exercise: Mock LANDINGS meeting (split into groups if necessary). Facilitator leads attendees through a modified schedule: Check-in (5 minutes) Opening prayer (5 minutes) Storytelling (20–25 minutes) Response to story (10 minutes) Break (5 minutes) Discussion: Why follow Jesus? (15 minutes) Wrap-up reflection (5 minutes) Intercessions / closing prayer (5 minutes)
12:45 p.m.	Reconvene for questions and comments on the mock meeting
1:00–1:30 p.m.	Lunch
1:30–2:45 p.m.	Planning your LANDINGS Ministry (Restart the DVD) Exercise: Group discussion (one hour) Set day and time for next meeting
3:00 p.m.	Closing prayer (DVD)

THE MINISTRY CERTIFICATE

Only those groups that have been properly trained in accordance with the guidelines provided are authorized to conduct the LANDINGS program.

After the training program has been successfully completed, please contact the LANDINGS office. The LANDINGS office will then issue the Ministry Certificate, which is good for five years and provides complimentary consultations with the LANDINGS ministry staff.

PART II

SCRIPT FOR LANDINGS TRAINING DVD

The complete running time of the training DVD is forty minutes and three seconds (40:03). As you can see below, each section of the script is keyed to the time when it begins on the DVD. This will enable you to quickly return to or review particular points.

LANDINGS LOGO (00:05)

OPENING (00:20)

On behalf of the Paulist Fathers, I would like to welcome you to the beginning of your LANDINGS journey. My name is Thomas Kane and I am the director of Paulist Reconciliation Ministries.

Hopefully, you will help others find the peace and enjoyment thousands have found through this dynamic program. LANDINGS is a unique approach to reconciliation ministry, giving those who are considering returning to the Church an insight into the actual faith lives of other Catholics. LANDINGS is not a discussion group or a class, but an experience of faith sharing.

More than anything else, LANDINGS is a ministry of compassionate listening. Some call listening the language of God. Over the course of the process, the LANDINGS team members and the returnees will each have ample opportunity to share together.

Welcome-team members are part of the faith-sharing process. You are not there to cure, teach, "fix," or sit in judgment. Compassionate listening works best when there is no interrupting, arguing, or commenting on what another has said.

LANDINGS has a highly successful track record. We urge you to follow the program as it is written. Its unique structure has been tested and proven effective by hundreds of groups over the past twenty years. LANDINGS is meant specifically for those discerning a return to the Church, and this format of storytelling and reflection works as a point of reentry for them.

If you respect the guidelines, enough of your Catholic identity will emerge to provide returnees with a genuine, balanced look into the heart of the Catholic faith as it is lived and experienced in your faith communities today. Confidentiality is essential to LANDINGS, especially to our spiritual autobiographies. Only in an atmosphere of trust will people speak openly and honestly of their lived beliefs. Those who feel comfortable returning to communion with the Church discover during the process that they are just as holy, just as smart, just as beloved by God—and just as Catholic—as the rest of us.

Each person's journey is special and sacred in the eyes of God. Trust the Holy Spirit and the process. We are confident you will grow in faith and understanding with the passing weeks and be for one another a sign of God's ongoing acceptance and unconditional love.

On behalf of the Paulist Fathers, may God bless you as you begin this grace-filled ministry. Happy LANDINGS!

INTRODUCTION (3:45)

Hello. My name is Anna LaNave and I am the national coordinator for LANDINGS International. I have the honor of leading you through this LANDINGS parish team training. As a parish LANDINGS facilitator myself for the past nine years, I know your involvement in this welcoming ministry will be as much a blessing for your team as it is for the returning Catholics who come to your LANDINGS group.

QUESTIONS? (4:12)

So relax. You may have a lot of fear and questions. Do you know enough to share your faith? Can you talk about your own story in front of total strangers? What if the returnees have questions you can't answer?

By the end of this training session, you will be ready and eager to start your LANDINGS ministry. Calling Catholics back to the Church is truly the work of the Holy Spirit. If you have been called to help with LANDINGS as a team member, God will equip you with all you need to love people back to the Church.

YOUR TEAM'S STORY (4:45)

What you will learn in LANDINGS is that everyone has a story—a life story that has brought you to this place today to be trained as a LANDINGS team member. It is important that you get to know your fellow team members. Please pause the video so your small group can answer these questions:

[Pause the video at the following list of questions.] (5:02)

- Who are you?
- Are you a returning Catholic yourself?
- If so, why did you leave the Church? What brought you back (person, event, experience)?
- And, finally, why do you think God is calling you to be part of LANDINGS?

[Restart the DVD when your group has finished.]

OPENING PRAYER EXPERIENCE (5:29)

Every LANDINGS meeting, after a time of check-in, starts with an opening prayer. We will be opening with a look at the parable of the Prodigal Son. Please have a member of your group prayerfully read Luke 15:11–32. Pay attention to the role of the father in the story.

[Pause the video at the following text and read the parable.] (5:50)

- How does the father welcome home his son?
- What is surprising about his response?

[Restart the DVD when your group has finished.]

A warm embrace, an invitation back to the table, a celebration: how can we, as LANDINGS team members, be Christ to the returnees that God brings us? It is simple. We must offer them a warm embrace with our words and actions, and love them back home. We are so happy that they are back that the angels are singing. We have missed them—they are part of our family, and they have come home. What we need to offer them is the realization that there is no such thing as a perfect Catholic, just all of us struggling to love God and neighbor more. We are companions on the journey. For the next eight weeks we will share our struggles as we listen to them share their stories.

As we close this opening section, join me in this prayer by Thomas Merton:

THE MERTON PRAYER (6:59)

"My Lord God, I have no idea where I am going. I do not see the road ahead of me. I cannot know for certain where it will end. Nor do I really know myself, and the fact that I think I am following your will does not mean that I am actually doing so. But I believe that the desire to please you does in fact please you. And I hope I have that desire in all that I am doing. I hope that I will never do anything apart from that desire. And I know that if I do this you will lead me by the right road, though I may know nothing about it. Therefore, I will trust you always though I may seem to be lost and in the shadow of death. I will not fear, for you are ever with me, and you will never leave me to face my perils alone."

—Thomas Merton, "Thoughts in Solitude" © Abbey of Gethsemani

THE 3 Cs TO BEING CHRIST TO THE RETURNEE (7:54)

How can I, as a LANDINGS team member, be Christ to the returnee?

There are 3 Cs to remember:

- *Compassionate listening*. Everyone wants to be heard and not judged. Give space to open up.
- *Conversation*. Be authentic and honest. Share your struggles and faith journey.
- *Community*. As you hear their stories, you will come to love the folks in your group. Usher them into the larger community of the parish. Invite them to Mass, soup suppers, and so on.

So it is simple. You don't have to be a theologian. As a team member, you offer a warm embrace. Then be a companion on the journey as they experience LANDINGS.

WHO IS OUR TARGET AUDIENCE FOR LANDINGS? (8:45)

According to the latest surveys, there are close to 65 million Catholics in the United States. Of those, only 36 percent attend Mass on a weekly basis. That means nearly two-thirds are inactive—over 40 million people—but still identify with the Catholic faith.

Why do people leave the Church? The reasons people stop practicing their faith are many: boredom, busy lives, divorce. Most don't leave angry with the Church, though many may have disagreements with the Church on issues of sexual morality or the role of women. Many don't leave angry: they're just ambivalent. They still pray and believe in God, but a majority (68 percent in one survey) don't think they need to attend Mass to be a "good Catholic."

Some young adults may not have attended Mass on a regular basis. As children of baby boomers, they may not understand what it is to be Catholic even if they completed their sacraments. Many are not sure they want to remain Catholic, but when they feel a spiritual void or get married or start having children of their own, they want to take another look at the Church of their childhood. They need a reentry ministry where they can be welcomed back and where they can reexamine their Catholic faith in a safe, nonjudgmental setting.

Perhaps your returnees are a lot like some of ours.

SHORT TESTIMONIES FROM RETURNEES (10:15)

A PASSIONATE LAY COORDINATOR / COFFEE MEETING (11:35)

A lay coordinator who is passionate about the success of LANDINGS is essential to the program. This person will be the face of the ministry to those looking to return.

If the coordinator is able, he or she should invite the returnee to meet for coffee before the LANDINGS session begins. For many, this will be the first "Church" representative they have spoken to in years. It is wonderful to have a friendly, encouraging conversation where they can ask their questions and tell their spiritual story for the first time.

You can then tell them about LANDINGS and the commitment it involves. It is important that the returnee understand that they should attend the entire program if possible, so that as each member tells his or her story there are familiar faces in the group. If they need to miss more than two meetings, consider inviting them to your next session. Continuity is important for the LANDINGS experience.

Do tell the returnee that they will be asked to tell their story to the group—as little or as much as they wish. This may seem intimidating to them, but you can tell them that they did a fine job of telling their story to you today during coffee! You then need to explain the schedule of session topics and dates, location for the meetings, and any closing celebration you have scheduled. Ask the returnee if they think that LANDINGS is right for them and if this is a good time in their life for LANDINGS. If they agree, give them a *Participant's Journal* and show them the topic for the first night.

THEIR OWN EXPERIENCES (13:18)

Point out that they should key in on the reflection questions. Remind them that though we do include some Church teaching for background, we are interested in their sharing their own experiences of the faith. There are no right or wrong answers as they share their reflections. They will find great encouragement in the discussions and in hearing the experiences of both the active Catholic team members as well as their fellow returnees.

SUNDAY LITURGY? (13:45)

Ask them if they have attended Mass recently. If they haven't, share with them a bulletin, and point out the different styles of liturgy at your parish. Encourage them to give Mass a try. Part of coming back to the Church is participating in the Sunday celebration again. The participants need to start going back and see how it feels. Don't pressure. A gentle nudge and invitation is what they might need. Many returnees, after the first few sessions, will make dates to meet each other for Mass (it is always nice to have someone to go with).

By the end of coffee, most returnees are at ease and eager for LANDINGS to begin. Most say that this is exactly what they were looking for as they discerned a return to the Church.

PREPARING FOR YOUR LANDINGS MEETING (14:28)

We will share with you the format for a LANDINGS meeting, then you will run your own "mock" meeting.

First, you have to prepare your location. Choose an enclosed room where you will not be disturbed. LANDINGS values confidentiality as an essential element, and nothing from the session should be shared with others outside the group. Set up a circle of chairs—no desks or tables. Your LANDINGS group should comprise a team of four to six welcome-team members and three to four returnees, with no more than ten in a group. The circle should surround a prayer table with a candle and open Bible. Have nametags available for the first few meetings.

ROLE OF THE FACILITATOR (15:09)

For this mock session, the facilitator is key for the working group and must be comfortable leading the group discussion and limiting each speaker to two minutes of sharing. Group dynamics are important to make everyone, even introverts, comfortable in the group, so the facilitator must be pastorally sensitive to the one sharing their story.

The facilitator will run the meeting, serve as timekeeper and discussion leader, and recruit someone to lead opening prayer.

MEETING SCHEDULE (15:39)

LANDINGS meeting schedule is an hour and a half to two hours each meeting for 8 to 10 weeks.

Meetings begin on time.

Check-in time (20 minutes)
Opening prayer (5 minutes)
Spiritual-journey storytelling (20–30 minutes)
Response to story (10 minutes)
Hospitality break (10 minutes)
Reflection on Catholic themes (30 minutes)
Housekeeping (5–10 minutes)
Closing prayer

End on time

THE LANDINGS MEETING STEP BY STEP (15:56)

CHECK-IN (16:06)

The meeting begins on time with the facilitator asking a check-in question, seeing how each person is doing, and hearing how last week's meeting impacted their lives. It is also a time to hear prayer requests that might have come up. Each person has about two minutes of sharing. This is not conversation, so no crosstalk.

OPENING PRAYER (17:01)

The check-in is then followed by an opening prayer, led by a different person each week. Guidelines are provided in the *Participant's Journal.* People are encouraged to be creative—to not merely recite a prayer, but to lead the group in reflection, possibly related to the evening's theme, with a period of silence or music.

SPIRITUAL-JOURNEY STORYTELLING (17:54)

After prayer, it is time for a team member (for the first few weeks, and then later a returnee) to tell their faith story—how God and the Church are influencing their lives. The storyteller should prepare to talk about twenty minutes. Guidelines on story preparation are contained in the *Participant's Journal*. Many like to write out notes before the session. The timekeeper should keep an eye on the clock and give a time warning.

In the group setting, compassionate listening is imperative. While the storyteller is talking, there should be no comments or questions. Active listening skills and eye contact are key. I have found that, for many returnees, telling their story is the most powerful part of LANDINGS. For the first time they can talk about their faith in a personal way in a Catholic setting. It is truly awesome to be blessed as a team member to hear how God has been active in their life up to now. Being asked to prepare their story assists the returnee to reflect on their life in a spiritual context. Healing can occur as past hurts are shared.

RESPONSE TO STORY (19:44)

After the storyteller finishes, each person has the opportunity to respond with a comment or to express thanks. Many listeners can relate to parts of the storyteller's journey, but it is important that the responders do not start to tell their own story—they will have another opportunity for sharing. After the response time, there is a ten-minute break for hospitality, during which people can share privately with the storyteller.

HOSPITALITY (20:49)

The hospitality is hosted by a different participant each week. We have found that the returnees enjoy serving each other in this way. Simple and healthy refreshments are important, especially since some participants have come straight from work to be at LANDINGS. This is also a time to socialize and take a break from the intensity of the storytelling. It is fun to be creative. One participant brought Mexican food for Cinco de Mayo, which was enjoyed by all.

REFLECTION ON CATHOLIC THEMES (21:37)

After the break, it is time for the reflection on Catholic topics. As our personal stories illustrate, the Catholic faith is not just the doctrines we believe and profess but a relationship between ourselves and a loving God. For Catholic Christians, the Church is more than a building or an institution. The Church is the People of God, the Body of Christ. Each of us is part of the Church, nourished on our spiritual journeys by Scripture and the sacraments, gifts of grace, and the Holy Spirit. The topics reintroduce us to our Catholic beliefs and help us to understand them as adults. Living authentically as a Catholic Christian may be quite a challenge, especially in our contemporary culture, but we are called to embrace this adventurous faith journey.

The themes for each week are the following:

I. Who Is God?
II. Why Follow Jesus?
III. The Holy Spirit and the Church
IV. Baptism and Confirmation
V. Eucharist and Liturgy
VI. Sin and Reconciliation
VII. Vocation
VIII. Suffering, Death, and Resurrection
IX. The Catholic Life (optional)
X. Christian Prayer (optional)

Each theme has a corresponding section in the *Participant's Journal.* The reflections will give you some theological background on the topic. Encourage the group to take some time to focus on the reflection questions (in italics in the journal). The evening's discussion will start with the facilitator asking one of these questions. Each person will be asked to give a two-minute reflection. Each person will want to take time before the meeting to prepare some thoughts to share. Remember, there are no wrong answers. Share your own lived experience of the faith. Be honest about your own questions and struggles. You may be surprised how many in your group may share the same concerns.

It is important that each person share their own experiences. It is amazing how, especially around topics like the Eucharist, Catholics when free to share are wonderfully orthodox in their faith. The contributions of the team members are especially encouraging as the returnees hear of others' spiritual journeys.

SHORT EUCHARIST REFLECTIONS (24:20)

THE SACRAMENT OF RECONCILIATION (25:24)

When dealing with Reconciliation, invite your pastor to join the group and facilitate the conversation. By this time, you are halfway through LANDINGS, and the group has bonded and feels comfortable with each other. They may be ready to return to the sacrament of Reconciliation, but need some reassurance. Our pastor loves to visit LANDINGS and always brings his calendar to make appointments for private reconciliation if any returnee wishes.

FACILITATOR REFLECTION (25:50)

After the discussion, the facilitator may wish to prepare a ten-minute personal reflection on the topic. Some references and sources are cited in the *Participant's Journal*. Remember that you are not a teacher or theologian. If serious questions come up—psychological, emotional, or spiritual—please encourage the returnee to go to your parish priest or a professional for help.

HOUSEKEEPING (27:04)

After the discussion, review assignments for next week: opening prayer, storyteller, hospitality host, and theme facilitator. If this is the first meeting, ask participants to sign up for the various tasks of the upcoming weeks. If anyone is going to be absent next week, it should be noted at this time.

CLOSING PRAYER (27:32)

For a closing prayer, you may include intercessions, following the model of the Prayers of the Faithful during Mass:

> **Individual**: *Let us pray for my mother who is ill: we pray to the Lord.*
> **Group**: *Lord, hear our prayer*.

After the intercessions, the group may recite together the Newman Prayer, which is included in the *Participant's Journal*.

THE NEWMAN PRAYER (28:00)

May [Christ] support us all the day long,
Til the shades lengthen, and the evening comes,
And the busy world is hushed, and the fever of life is over,
And our work is done!
Then, in His mercy, may He give us
Safe lodging, and a holy rest, and peace at the last!

—Blessed John Henry Cardinal Newman

MOCK LANDINGS MEETING

Now it is time for your mock meeting. Take the next hour and a half to run through a LANDINGS meeting. Select a facilitator, opening prayer leader, storyteller, and theme facilitator. Guidelines are provided in the *Participant's Journal*. You may want to a start with the Preamble and follow the schedule on the inside of the *Participant's Journal*. I suggest the topic "Who Is Jesus?" for your reflection [correction: "Why Follow Jesus?—*ed*.].

Keep to the schedule, timekeeper!

Pause this video and return after your mock LANDINGS meeting. After the meeting, you may want to take a short break for a meal or snack.

[Pause the video at LANDINGS Logo.] (29:00)

AFTER YOUR MOCK MEETING (29:06)

Welcome back. How did your meeting go? Did you keep to the schedule, or did you go way overtime? It is important to respect everyone's time, keeping your meeting to its schedule. If you have questions, I encourage you to read the LANDINGS program guide [which is Part III of this book]. Feel free to contact us at the LANDINGS International office, where we would be happy to provide you with assistance.

I have facilitated LANDINGS for close to a decade, and I assure you that once your first session is under way you will understand the format—and it is quite simple. Stick to the guidelines provided. LANDINGS is an experience of faith sharing and has been successful for twenty years. Let the Holy Spirit work and you will be amazed at the blessings LANDINGS can bring to your returnees and most surprisingly to your team and parish.

CELEBRATE (29:53)

Once your LANDINGS session has come to a close, and everyone has told their story, host a celebration evening. Some LANDINGS groups go on a retreat together; others have a simple home Mass, followed by a potluck meal. Many will have availed themselves of sacramental Reconciliation. It is powerful to end your time together with a liturgy. Encourage people to testify to what LANDINGS has meant to them and encourage them to think about their involvement in the parish.

I also give the returnees a simple rosary or spiritual book geared toward their interests. Approach returnees whom you think would like to join you as a LANDINGS team member for your next session. Recent returnees are valuable team members with fresh stories and enthusiasm.

PLANNING YOUR LANDINGS MARKETING (30:43)

Now that your team has been trained, it is time to schedule your first session and plan outreach to the inactive and returning Catholics in your community. I encourage you to refer to the *Coordinator's Guide*, with its checklists and helpful marketing tools. Most LANDINGS sessions are run twice a year in the fall and spring. Run advertising for new groups in the summer months and at Christmas and Lent.

Remember that your returnees are not necessarily sitting in your pews, but are out there. Pulpit announcements by your pastor, bulletin announcements, and pew cards are helpful in getting the word out to your parish community so they can encourage their friends and relatives to give LANDINGS a try. Referrals by priests and parish staff are also critical to the success of your ministry. Be creative. St. Jude's in Jacksonville, Arkansas, aided by marketing rep Jeffrey Stewart, ran this ad on the local TV station.

JACKSONVILLE AD (31:45)

Your marketing campaign should last about six weeks. Use an appropriate e-mail address like LANDINGS@stcharleschurch.org. How about a flyer and tear-off sheet at all the local coffee houses?

Signage is also very important. You should consider a sign outside your church. Avoid the words *lapsed* or *ex-Catholics*, but consider "Inactive Catholics—Take another look," or "Welcome Returning Catholics—Come Home to St. Charles" and the Web site of the church.

It is the Internet that will attract the most returnees. If your parish has a Web site, make up a LANDINGS page with a link to a banner ad on the home page. Don't put too much information on the page, as you want them to contact you so you can make that personal connection. It takes a lot of courage to e-mail the church after years away.

Don't make it hard for the returnee to find you. The *Coordinator's Guide* has a sample Web and home page that we use at my parish. Advertise it next to RCIA, such as "Return to the Church again," with a link to LANDINGS. We have this new marketing video that you may use to advertise LANDINGS.

LANDINGS MARKETING AD FOR YOUR OWN WEB SITE (33:28)

NOTE: This ad is included on your DVD in a separate file. It can be taken directly off the DVD and posted on your Web site.

EXPECTATIONS (36:57)

Set your expectations low in terms of numbers. Most LANDINGS groups have about three to four returnees per session, and that is perfect for the format of this program. It is a quiet and confidential ministry. If you have just one returnee, don't be disappointed. Go ahead and run your session with your team. For that one returnee, the LANDINGS session can be life-changing. If you have a permanent presence on your parish Web site, and receive inquiries between sessions or after the session has started, respond to them and keep the information for the next session.

Now pause this video and have your team discuss how you will market LANDINGS in your parish.

[Pause the video to discuss marketing.] (37:45)

WHAT NEXT? (37:52)

Many LANDINGS groups are very sorry to see their session end. After eight weeks, the friendships that have been forged are lifelong. Encourage your returnees to get involved in the parish right away. If they feel like they need more formation, I encourage returnees to volunteer as an RCIA sponsor, or join Cursillo or a Bible study group. LANDINGS is only the beginning of their journey back.

We at LANDINGS International will be praying for your ministry. If you have to order more materials or have questions, please feel free to contact us. We want to hear how LANDINGS worked in your community. It is exciting for us to know that, by opening your heart to those away from the Church, you are participating in the work of reconciliation—the mission of the Church—to spread the love of Christ throughout our world, especially to our brother and sister Catholics who are missing from the table.

Blessings to you as you embark on this adventure of LANDINGS. In closing, please join me in a LANDINGS prayer:

LANDINGS PRAYER (39:01)

Lord, let me welcome all my sisters and brothers
with the arms of Christ.
May I listen to their stories
with the openness of Christ.
And may I embrace them
with the Love of Christ.
Through my hospitality,
may they once more
call the Church their home. Amen.
—Richard Chilson, CSP

FOR MATERIALS AND INFORMATION:

Contact LANDINGS International
LANDINGSdc@yahoo.com
202-269-2550

LANDINGS Logo

CREDITS

Anna LaNave—Scriptwriter/Host
Father Thomas Kane, CSP—Producer
Blue Rock Productions, Baltimore, Maryland

Paulist Reconciliation Ministries Logo

END OF TRAINING SCRIPT (40:03)

PART III

LANDINGS PROGRAM GUIDE

BEFORE THE START OF THE SESSION

A week before the new session starts, the program facilitator should host the welcome team to review and prepare for the first meeting, as by now it will have been several weeks since the team's training, or several months since the last session. The number of team members needed per session should be based on the number of returnees. The ideal LANDINGS group is eight to ten people. If there are four returnees, there should be no more than six welcome-team members, including the facilitator. If there are six returnees, reduce the welcome team to four members, so that the overall group size is not overwhelming. If there are more than six returnees, it might be best to form two separate groups. Team members should commit to the entire session.

Your agenda for this pre-session meeting covers many points. Use the following checklist as a guide and add to it as you need:

PRE-SESSION CHECKLIST

√ Allow check-in time as usual to get back into the LANDINGS spirit. Ask each welcome-team member: "How have you seen God work in your life since the last session?"

√ Share the session calendar with the welcome team.

√ Assign two team members as the opening prayer leader and hospitality host for the first meeting.

√ Assign two team members as the storyteller for the first two meetings. These stories shared by welcome-team members in the first few weeks will serve as a model for returnees.

√ Assign a different team member to lead the reflection topic and reflection wrap-up for each week. Schedule the entire session now, so that team members can prepare for their turn.

√ Assign a team member as the "backup" storyteller for week 6 on sin and reconciliation. Although it is not recommended that the pastor or a pastoral staff member participate in every meeting, it is helpful to have the pastor participate in meeting 6 on the sacrament of Reconciliation. This comes toward the middle of the session. The returnees will be comfortable with each other by then and may be ready to seek individual sacramental Reconciliation or to ask the pastor questions. Ask the storyteller for that night if he or she would be comfortable with the pastor sitting in. If he or she would not be comfortable, have the pastor arrive after the hospitality break. If the storyteller would rather not speak that night at all, have your backup team member prepared to share his or her own story.

√ Verify with the welcome-team members that they know the meeting-room assignment(s), time, place, and directions of the first meeting.

As the first meeting draws closer, don't forget the following details, many of which were also on the checklist for arranging the training day:

PRE-MEETING CHECKLIST

√ Contact all returnees with meeting information: time, place, and directions.

√ Encourage any returnee who now seems reluctant, anxious, fearful, or indecisive about attending LANDINGS.

√ Double-check the room assignment. If you were unable to get the same room(s) you used for training, check that this is also a quiet section of the building.

√ Have a small prayer table, candle, crucifix, and Bible readily available.

√ Make copies of the week-by-week schedule by date for the entire session. To do this, photocopy the next section, titled "Meeting Schedule," fill in the days and dates of your actual session, and then make copies of this sheet for the group. This is especially important when there are exceptions to the schedule, such as a week that will be skipped because of a holiday. All exceptions should be noted on the schedule that you hand out to both returnees and team members.

√ Ensure that there are enough copies of the *Participant's Journal*, prayer cards, and any other materials you plan to share.

√ Provide nametags and pens to use at the first few meetings.

√ Bring a watch for timekeeping!

MEETING SCHEDULE

The meetings focus on sharing our faith stories and reflecting on Catholic themes. Below is the format for every meeting, as well as the dates we'll meet. Additional information for each section is provided in the *Participant's Journal*.

Program facilitator begins all meetings on time!

1. Check-in time: 20 minutes
2. Opening prayer leader: 5 minutes
3. Spiritual journey storytelling: 20–30 minutes
4. Response to story: 10 minutes
5. Hospitality break: 10 minutes
6. Reflection on Catholic themes: 20–25 minutes

   I. Who is God?
   II. Why Follow Jesus?
   III. The Holy Spirit and the Church
   IV. Baptism and Confirmation
   V. Eucharist and Liturgy
   VI. Sin and Reconciliation
   VII. Vocation
   VIII. Suffering, Death, and Resurrection
   IX. The Catholic Life (optional week)
   X. Christian Prayer (optional week; may also be any other theme of interest to the group)

7. Program facilitator's or leader's reflection: 10 minutes
8. Housekeeping: 5 minutes
9. Closing prayer

May [Christ] support us all the day long,
Til the shades lengthen, and the evening comes,
And the busy world is hushed, and the fever of life is over,
And our work is done!
Then, in His mercy, may He give us
Safe lodging, and a holy rest, and peace at the last!

—Blessed John Henry Cardinal Newman

THE FIRST LANDINGS MEETING

Here are the program facilitator's duties during the actual first meeting, many of which carry over for the whole session:

- Begin on time to end on time! Resist the urge to wait for latecomers. Allow latecomers to slip unobtrusively into the circle.
- Include everyone in early structured small talk during check-in.
- Read aloud the Preamble from the *Participant's Journal* to get in the spirit of LANDINGS.
- Introduce LANDINGS as a ministry of *compassionate listening*. The group honors their fellow members by being respectful listeners to each other's spiritual journey. The Holy Spirit has brought them to LANDINGS. The meetings must be sacred, safe spaces for all to share and to be authentic with each other.
- Emphasize compassionate listening as *confidential listening*, so that everything said during the LANDINGS session is confidential and will not be repeated outside the group. Again, the meetings must be sacred, safe spaces in order for all to share and to be authentic with each other.
- Review the LANDINGS session schedule and meeting schedule with the returnees.
- Send around a sign-up sheet at the break to solicit volunteers for the storyteller, opening prayer leader, and hospitality host for the remaining meetings. Have team members fill in the vacancies as necessary. Normally the program facilitator leads the opening of the LANDINGS meetings, serves as timekeeper, and shares these other roles, as needed.
- Plan your last meeting's celebration. To close the time together, many LANDINGS groups celebrate a home Mass or have a dinner. Some even plan on going on retreat.

TIMEKEEPING

During the first meeting, introduce the concept of time management. This concept often meets with resistance, but experience indicates how crucial it is to the success of LANDINGS. Facilitators often report how much they come to appreciate this part of the process.

If the facilitator is unable to do this task, a timekeeper from the welcome team should be appointed, someone who is not intimidating and can carry out this responsibility.

WHY USE TIME MANAGEMENT?

- Most people have little experience with timekeeping and need assistance.
- Timekeeping will limit extroverts and involve introverts.
- Starting and ending on time—not only for the whole meeting, but also for its individual sections—helps the group learn to respect everyone's time.

THE TIMEKEEPER'S TASKS

Most sections call for a maximum speaking time of two minutes per person. This applies to sharing during check-in, responding to the storyteller, and responding to the reflection questions on the theme.

Time limits on storytelling itself are a little more flexible. Generally the group is allowed twenty to thirty minutes, depending on whether the meeting is ninety minutes or two hours. If possible, a two-hour meeting is recommended so the group does not feel rushed. For the storyteller, indicate when there are five minutes left for the story, so he or she can begin to wrap it up. But be pastorally sensitive. If the story is especially moving at that point, give a little more time, but make sure there is also time for responses before the break.

Now let's move beyond these overall tips to look at each section of a LANDINGS meeting.

CHECK-IN

Begin on time! If someone comes in late during this part of the meeting, repeat the question for him or her so that everyone has a chance to speak. This is a time to see how everyone is doing, and what kind of mood each person is in. Use one of the questions in the *Participant's Journal*. Emphasize the need to share how the participants saw God active in their lives this past week.

Be careful to limit each person's input to about two minutes. Go around in a circle so all can respond (people can "pass," if they would rather not participate). Be alert to the purpose of the check-in and do not let anyone go off on a tangent. Keep the conversation focused on the topic. If something serious has happened to a member this past week, go ahead and give a little more time to hear about it. Be sure to include an intercession for that person in the closing prayer.

OPENING PRAYER

Prayer time should cultivate a peace and calm that enhances the group's ability to be receptive to the upcoming story. At the first session, it is important that the team member leading the prayer follow the format suggested in the *Participant's Journal*. Encourage the next opening prayer leader, who should be a returnee, to give some thought to preparation. Avoid criticizing the way someone leads the prayer.

STORYTELLING

The group will grow to understand the sacredness of the storyteller sharing his or her life story. And many storytellers will find it very freeing to share some of their joys and struggles with God and the Church with others who are willing to walk with them on their journey.

As we said earlier, recruit team members to share their stories for the first and second sessions to model the process for the returnees. At the first meeting, ask for volunteers from the returnees by using a sign-up sheet. The returnees should sign up first. The members of the welcome team can then fill in the weeks where the storytelling slot is empty. Both the returnees and the welcome-team members may tell their stories, though returnees should take priority.

GUIDING THE STORYTELLER

Schedule the returnees' stories several weeks in advance. This gives them time for preparation and reflection. Tell them to use the guidelines in the *Participant's Journal* to help prepare their stories. Encourage using the writing space in the booklet if they need to write it out or to take notes.

Explain that their story should take twenty to thirty minutes and that, as a timekeeper, you will give a signal when there are five minutes remaining. However, make it clear that the storyteller should not stop abruptly at your signal, but begin to wind down. During the actual storytelling, use your judgment to give a five-minute extension if needed.

Remind the group about confidentiality.

RESPONSE TO THE STORY

In order for the group to respond with compassion to the storyteller, they must first learn to be compassionate listeners:

- Listen carefully and give the storyteller their full attention
- Nod their heads or convey encouragement in other ways
- Maintain easy eye contact with the storyteller
- Be still and do not interrupt

When the storyteller is finished, members of the group should respond by offering brief encouragement and thanking the person for his or her story.

Invite the group to reflect on what moved them as individual listeners. Remind them not to question, offer advice, or correct. Their comments should be restricted to how the story touched them and should not lead into their telling their own stories at this time. The focus should remain on the storyteller.

When feedback runs down, ask the storyteller how he or she is feeling and if he or she wants more response from the group.

When you feel the time is right, break for hospitality, saying something like, "We can continue our responses during hospitality." Some may approach the storyteller for a private comment during this time.

A day or so after the meeting, call on the storyteller. Inquire how he or she is doing. Offer thanks, assurance, and appreciation.

REFLECTION ON CATHOLIC THEMES

As mentioned earlier, before the session starts, assign reflection leaders for each week's topic from the team members. The leader will review the topic and reflection questions for the week and select some questions to start the discussion. Also invite your pastor to serve as the reflection leader for the topic of Reconciliation. By that time, your group will be halfway through the program, and many may be ready to consider availing themselves of the sacrament. The pastor's presence allows the returnees to ask questions or to make an appointment with him, if they wish.

For the other meetings, the reflection leader for that week should call everyone back from the hospitality break to the circle to introduce the theme, following the timeline in the *Participant's Journal*. He or she should ask the group one of the questions from the *Journal* that follow each theme. Group members should then comment on the question for two to three minutes each. You may meet resistance with time limits; hold your ground. Preserving the structure unlocks a marvelous level of trust and sharing.

The leader will invite each member to offer his or her personal reflection on the evening's topic. Everyone should be given the chance to answer, and also the choice to pass. There should be no crosstalk, which occurs when several members in the group start their own private conversation while others listen in. If this happens, intervene politely to get the conversation back on track, and see that everyone—returnees and team members—has a chance to make a contribution.

If the reflection ends sooner than expected, the leader should proceed to another of the theme's questions from the *Participant's Journal* or should accept a question from the group. If the leader doesn't, be prepared to ask a second question yourself. Maintain the courtesy of rotating within the group rather than allowing anyone to dominate the meeting. Encourage people to speak openly and honestly without being criticized or judged. Trust the Holy Spirit and the group wisdom to guide these reflections.

You may want to make a copy of the following to give to the welcome-team members as guidance as reflection leaders.

LEADER'S REFLECTION

PREPARATION

Prepare the theme for the week ahead by reading the reflection in the *Participant's Journal*. Read the additional resources and related Scripture quotations that follow the reflection. Look up any of the recommended resources that you might find helpful.

Read the list of suggested questions for that theme. Pick one of the questions or develop your own for the group to reflect and comment on. Prepare a ten-minute wrap-up reflection, based on your own experiences as well as the Church teaching discussed in the *Participant's Journal*.

AT THE MEETING

Introduce the topic and ask the question you've chosen. Go around the circle and allow two- to three-minute reflections from each member. He or she may pass if they wish. Be prepared with a second question if the group's comments end quickly.

For your wrap-up reflection, speak from your heart as well as your head. The point is not to teach theology, but to reacquaint returnees with the traditions and teachings of the Church. The reflection should share your lived experience of the Catholic faith, coming from the heart and the head. Don't be afraid to share your own doubts or struggles in the storytelling. People will be at different places in their faith journey around these themes. Respect their views and their place in the returning process.

HOUSEKEEPING

After the reflection time, the program facilitator reviews the assignments for the next week. If any of the roles of opening prayer leader, storyteller, hospitality host, and reflection leader still need to be filled, strongly urge people to volunteer, especially anyone who has hung back until now. Also announce the topic for next week's reflection.

During the week, be sure to contact the group with a reminder a few days before the meeting to again review the assignments and the theme. Ask the participants to jot down a thought or two in their *Participant's Journal* in preparation for what they will share.

CLOSING PRAYER

Close each LANDINGS meeting in prayer. If the group wishes, they may include intercessions, using the model of the Prayers of the Faithful during Mass. For example:

Individual: *Let us pray for my aunt who is sick and also for all those in hospitals and nursing homes; we pray to the Lord.*
All: *Lord, hear our prayer.*

The facilitator should note when there are no more intercessions. The meeting closes with the Newman Prayer, which appears above and also in the *Participant's Journal*.

THE LAST LANDINGS MEETING

As you near the end of the program, prepare the closing celebration for LANDINGS. If someone will be absent for the celebration, it should be noted at this time.

Make the group aware of special events or liturgies happening over the next few weeks in your faith community that they might be interested in. Some welcome-team members may also be willing to mention which Sunday liturgy they usually attend and offer to sit with the returnees. Both these things invite returnees into a deeper relation with the community and the Church.

Distribute evaluation sheets (see the *Coordinator's Guide*) at the start of the last meeting. Have everyone complete the form. Later copy the evaluations for your review and send the originals to the LANDINGS office. The returnees will then be eligible to receive future newsletters and information on other spiritual programs. LANDINGS is just a first step in a lifelong spiritual journey. Hopefully the program will help the returnees feel more comfortable with the Catholic faith and encourage them to become an active member of the Church community.

At your final meeting, encourage all participants to reflect on their LANDINGS experience and on the next steps in their journey. Are they ready to get involved in the community? Are they still unsure and need more conversation? Encourage those eager to share their experience to serve on a LANDINGS team. Recently returned Catholics can be a real encouragement to others just starting their journey.

FINAL CELEBRATION

Conclude the program with a celebration. After journeying with each other for eight weeks, the returnees will find it is good to celebrate with each other and share their LANDINGS experiences, possibly by going on a weekend retreat or attending a Sunday liturgy together. Many groups ask the pastoral staff for a special liturgy, concluding with a simple meal. Encourage family and friends to join in.

When giving a gift is possible, a rosary or spiritual book is a fitting welcome-back present from the faith community. Many returnees are sad to see LANDINGS end, and a closing celebration completes this first step of a lifelong spiritual journey. The end of LANDINGS is not the end of their spiritual journey but a beautiful beginning to their life again as members of the Catholic community.

POINTERS FOR A SUCCESSFUL MEETING

- Begin and end on time. Respect those who arrive on time. Keep an eye on the clock.
- Make sure that check-in takes no more than twenty minutes. Facilitators should gently curtail talkers and remind them that they'll have another opportunity to socialize during the break.
- Help the group quiet down and center on God's presence by not rushing the transition from checking-in to the opening prayer by immediately turning the group over to the prayer leader. A different person should lead the prayer each week.
- Encourage all to share their spiritual journeys, but force no one to do so.
- Remind returnees and welcome-team members alike that everything said in LANDINGS should remain confidential.
- Make sure there is adequate response to the week's story, as little-to-no response from the group could make the storyteller feel that he or she does not share in their common experience—to the point of being discouraged enough to stop their journey back home. It's useful to have a couple of questions to ask the group *only* when you need to elicit more response: for example, "What part of the story that was shared with you tonight are you most grateful for having heard? What do you think was the most difficult (or courageous or XXX) part of this story to live through?"

- Be alert to comments that take the focus away from the storyteller. Watch the clock to make sure that you have time for a break. Remind people that they may continue to respond to the storyteller privately during the break.
- Invite the returnees and welcome-team members to sign up to bring refreshments. This will help all to feel like they are sharing the gift of hospitality with their groups. It's also a nonthreatening way for returnees to participate.
- Allow the reflection leader for the evening to call the group back from break, rather than doing it yourself and then turning the group over to him or her. This is a better transition for his or her handling this next part of the meeting.
- Be aware of anyone whom the reflection leader might have overlooked and who hasn't had a chance to answer the question or to pass. Gently try to include the person before the wrap-up reflection begins.
- Defer answering difficult questions until the following week in order to first talk to the pastor. Any returnee having special pastoral needs (annulments, reconciliation, counseling, and so on) should be encouraged to meet with the pastor or a staff member.
- Contact anyone who misses a meeting and show interest in them.

* * *

After much experience, we can say: LANDINGS works! If you follow the process and are alert to these guidelines and the Holy Spirit, LANDINGS will be a wonderful experience for your community!

PAULIST PRESS

ISBN: 978-0-8091-9686-9

51995

9 780809 196869